AMAZING QUESTIONS KIDS ASK ABOUT GOD

AMAZING
QUESTIONS
KIDS ASK ABOUT
God

DAVID R. VEERMAN, M.DIV.

JAMES C. GALVIN, ED.D.

JAMES C. WILHOIT, PH.D.

DARYL J. LUCAS

RICHARD OSBORNE

Tyndale House
Publishers, Inc.
Carol Stream,
Illinois

TYNDALE is a registered trademark of Tyndale House Publishers, Inc.

Tyndale's quill logo is a trademark of Tyndale House Publishers, Inc.

Amazing Questions Kids Ask about God

Copyright © 1992 by The Livingstone Corporation and Lightwave Publishing, Inc. All rights reserved.

Illustrations by Lil Esau. "Jason and Max" © 1989 Impartation Idea, Inc.

Produced with the assistance of The Livingstone Corporation

Unless otherwise noted, Scripture quotations are taken from *The Simplified Living Bible,* copyright © 1990 by KNT Charitable Trust. All rights reserved. Used by permission.

Scripture quotations marked NIV are from the *Holy Bible*, New International Version. Copyright © 1973, 1978, 1984 International Bible Society. Used by permission of Zondervan Publishing House. Scripture quotations marked NRSV are from the New Revised Standard Version Bible. Copyright © 1989 Division of Christian Education of the National Council of the Churches of Christ in the United States of America. Scripture quotations marked KJV are taken from the *Holy Bible,* King James Version.

ISBN-13: 978-1-4143-0799-2
ISBN-10: 1-4143-0799-3

Printed in the United States of America

10 09 08 07 06
 6   5   4   3   2   1

CONTENTS

INTRODUCTION

Children are filled with questions as they begin to discover the world and learn how to ask. Some of their questions are simple and easy to answer, like, "Do I have to eat these peas?" and "Can I stay up?" But many of their queries are complex and seem impossible to answer, especially when children ask why. And when they move into the spiritual realm, the questions can be downright profound.

Of course, an easy response to anything children ask (a response that is used, unfortunately, by many parents) is, "Just because!" or "Because I said so!" That may be a response, but it's not an answer, and it is certainly unsatisfying to the child.

Instead, parents should handle their children's questions with loving care, seeing them for what they are—bubbles of curiosity, fresh moments of honesty, and exciting opportunities to teach.

That's why this book was written, to give parents help in answering their children's questions about God, the Bible, life after death, Jesus, and other spiritual issues.

The questions in this book are real; that is, they were really asked by boys and girls. Out of scores of questions, 101 were chosen to answer. And speaking of answers, each one has been carefully thought through and crafted, not as the last, exhaustive word on the subject, but as an honest answer for young, inquiring minds.

Related questions, key verses, and other Bible references are also included with each question.

As you answer your child's questions, remember to . . .

- Look for the question behind the question. For example, when a little boy asks, "Does the devil have claws?" (question 73), he probably wants to know, "Can the devil hurt me?"
- Be careful about making up an answer when you don't have one and when the Bible is silent (for example, "What does my angel do?"—question 71). Too often, children will later lump faith with other stories and superstitions they've been taught and then discovered were false. Be honest with your answers. If you don't have one, say so. Or suggest that you look for the answer together.
- Be ready for follow-up questions. Your answer may lead to more questions. That's the mark of a good answer—it makes the child think.
- Make your answers concrete. Children think in very literal and concrete terms, so abstract concepts such as "heaven," "justification," and "God's will" are difficult for them to understand until their ability to think abstractly naturally develops. But children can learn to pray, obey what God wants, and read and memorize the Bible.
- Always take children's questions seriously, even when they sound funny to you. It's amazing what little eyes see and little ears hear. One little girl ended a prayer with, "In Jesus' name, M&M." Another one asked about "the turtle's life" after hearing her father talk about "eternal life."

Jesus said, "Let the little children come to me. Don't stop them. For the Kingdom of Heaven belongs to such as these" (Matthew 19:14). We can unintentionally hinder children by ignoring their questions, not taking the time to answer them, or not taking them seriously. We can also hinder children by our own example, living as if faith in Christ does not make a difference.

May God help us as we tenderly care for these precious lives he has entrusted to us.

CREATION

Q: WHY DID GOD CREATE THE WORLD?

A: God created the world and everything in it because he enjoys making things, and he wanted to be with us. God created people because he wanted to have friends, men and women, boys and girls, with whom he could share his love. He created the world for them to live in and enjoy.

KEY VERSES: *In the beginning God created the heavens and the earth. . . . Then God looked over all that he had made. It was excellent in every way. (Genesis 1:1, 31)*

RELATED VERSES: *Genesis 1:1–2:1; Psalm 19:1; Isaiah 45:7*

RELATED QUESTIONS: *Why did God rest when all he did was speak? Why did God create water when there was milk?*

NOTE TO PARENTS: *This question is a good opportunity to tell your children that God's plan involves them. God created the world and everything in it—including your children—so that he could have people to love.*

Q: HOW DID GOD CREATE THE EARTH?

A: Whenever we make something, like a craft, a drawing, or a sand castle, we have to start with special materials, like clay, string, glue, paper, crayons, and sand. We can't even imagine creating something out of nothing—by just saying the words and making it appear. But God is so powerful that he can do what is impossible for us. That includes making anything he wants, even creating things from nothing. That's what it means to be God—he can do anything.

KEY VERSES: *Before anything else existed, there was God's Son. He was the Word, and he was with God. He has always been alive and is himself God. He created everything there is. Nothing exists that he didn't make. (John 1:1-3)*

RELATED VERSES: *Genesis 1:1-2; Hebrews 1:10; 2 Peter 3:5-6*

RELATED QUESTIONS: *Why did it take God six days to create the world? What was everything like before God created the world?*

Q: WERE THERE DINOSAURS ON THE ARK?

A: Dinosaurs are popular today. They're on television and in the comics. We even have dinosaur stuffed toys. Scientists say that these unusual animals lived and became extinct over a hundred million years ago, so it's natural to wonder where they fit into the Bible. Most Bible experts believe that dinosaurs died out many years before the great flood that we read about in Genesis. So there wouldn't have been any dinosaurs around to put on the ark. Another reason we don't read about dinosaurs in the Bible is that the Bible wasn't written to tell us everything. It's not a science textbook. The Bible tells us about people and God's plan for our life.

KEY VERSES: *[God is speaking] "Look at Behemoth, which I made just as I made you; it eats grass like an ox. Its strength is in its loins, and its power in the muscles of its belly. It makes its tail stiff like a cedar; the sinews of its thighs are knit together. Its bones are tubes of bronze, its limbs like bars of iron." (Job 40:15-19, NRSV)*

RELATED VERSES: *Genesis 7:1-24; John 1:3*

RELATED QUESTIONS: *Why don't we have dinosaurs today? Why aren't dinosaurs mentioned in the Bible? Where do dinosaurs fit into the Bible? Were there dinosaurs around with Adam and Eve?*

NOTE TO PARENTS: *The Bible doesn't mention dinosaurs, but it does say that God created everything (John 1:3). Some verses, like the one about Behemoth, talk about animals almost as big as dinosaurs.*

Q: WHY DID GOD MAKE MOSQUITOES?

A: When we're being attacked by mosquitoes, it's easy to wonder why God made pests and other animals that can harm us. When God created the world, it was perfect. Only after sin entered the picture did animals and human beings become enemies, causing humans to protect and defend themselves. So now mosquitoes try to feed off of us. They, in turn, become food for birds and bats. In the future, in the new heaven and new earth, animals won't hurt people or each other.

KEY VERSES: *In that day the wolf and the lamb will lie down together. And the leopard and goats will be at peace. Calves and fat cattle will be safe among lions. And a little child shall lead them all. The cows will graze among bears. Cubs and calves will lie down side by side. And lions will eat grass like the cows. Babies will crawl safely among deadly snakes. And a little child who puts his hand into a nest of adders will not be hurt. Nothing will hurt or destroy in all my holy mountain. And as the waters fill the sea, the earth will be full of the knowledge of the Lord. (Isaiah 11:6-9)*

RELATED VERSES: *Genesis 3:17-19; Romans 8:19-22*

RELATED QUESTIONS: *Why did God make bugs that bother us? Why did God make animals that we can't eat?*

Q: WHY DO SHARKS EAT PEOPLE?

A:
Sharks attack people because they are meat-eaters. When they are hungry, they will attack anything that looks good to eat. Sharks don't go looking for people to attack—they just react to what comes near them. The best thing to do is to be smart and stay away from sharks. When we go where we shouldn't go, we get into trouble—like walking in poison ivy or playing in a thunderstorm. There are dangers in the world, and we should be careful to avoid them.

KEY VERSES: *For wisdom will enter your heart, and knowledge will be pleasant to your soul. Discretion will protect you, and understanding will guard you. (Proverbs 2:10-11, NIV)*

RELATED VERSES: *Genesis 3:17-19; Numbers 21:6; Deuteronomy 32:24; Jeremiah 8:17; Ezekiel 34:25; Matthew 10:16*

RELATED QUESTIONS: *Why did God make animals that harm us? Why did God create poison ivy and poisonous plants?*

NOTE TO PARENTS: *The question of why God made animals that can harm us is answered earlier in Question 4. The answer according to Scripture is that we live in a sinful world (Genesis 3:14-19).*

Q: IF GOD MADE SPIDERS, WHY DO PEOPLE SQUISH THEM?

A: God created spiders just as he made all the other animals. But there's a great difference between animals and human beings. People are created in God's image and are supposed to take care of all creation—including all animals and plants. God put people in charge of creation, but this does not mean we can harm and kill for fun or destroy the world as we please. We can kill animals and plants for food and to control their population; we can remove or kill spiders, insects, and so forth that threaten us or make it difficult for us to live. But we should be kind to animals when possible and take good care of the world.

KEY VERSE: *And God blessed them and told them, "Multiply and fill the earth and subdue it. You are masters of the fish and birds and all the animals." (Genesis 1:28)*

RELATED VERSES: *Genesis 1:20-25; Proverbs 12:10; Acts 10:9-16*

NOTE TO PARENTS: *Some children want to hurt animals, while others want to be compassionate. God's desire is for us to be compassionate and wise rulers of all animal life (Proverbs 12:10). This should not be taken to such an extreme that we think eating meat is wrong. God has provided animals as a source of food and has given us permission to eat meat (see Acts 10).*

Q: WHY DID GOD MAKE PEOPLE RED AND YELLOW, BLACK AND WHITE?

7

A: Can you imagine a world in which everyone looked the same—the same height, weight, color of hair, length of nose, color of eyes, size of ears, and color of skin? That would be boring—and how would we tell people apart? Instead, God created all kinds and colors of people. Some are tall; some are short; some are brown; some are pink; some have straight black hair; some have curly red hair. They are all special to God. Don't you just love the differences and what makes you special? God does!

KEY VERSE: *In this new life your nation or race or education or social group means nothing. Christ is what matters, and he has been given to all. (Colossians 3:11)*

RELATED VERSES: *Jeremiah 13:23; Acts 17:26*

RELATED QUESTION: *How did people get different color skin when Adam and Eve were only one color?*

Q: DID GOD MAKE PEOPLE IN OUTER SPACE?

8

A: Although people may talk about creatures in outer space, no one really knows whether there is life on other planets. Most of the talk about other life forms comes from make-believe movies and what people imagine *might* be true. But if there is life in other parts of the universe, God is in charge of it because God is in charge of the whole universe. God created *everything,* and he is the God of all life everywhere, no matter where it may be.

KEY VERSE: *Christ created everything in Heaven and earth. He created the things we can see and the things we can't see. All kings and kingdoms, rulers and powers were made by Christ. He made them for his own use and glory. (Colossians 1:16)*

RELATED VERSES: *Genesis 1:1; 1 Chronicles 29:11-12*

RELATED QUESTIONS: *Are there aliens in outer space? Why did God make Mars and Jupiter?*

Q: HOW DOES GOD MAKE THE SUN AND MOON GO UP AND DOWN?

9

A: God made powerful laws to govern the universe. These laws control the movements of the sun, moon, earth, and other planets and stars. For example, one law called "gravity" draws objects toward each other. Other natural laws control the weather. Many forces determine whether the day will be sunny or cloudy, warm or cold, such as the heat from the sun, the currents in the ocean, the wind, and many others. God set up the rules that make all these forces work together. And because God controls the entire universe, he can interrupt the laws if he wants to—bring rain to dry land or bright sunshine to flooded areas. How powerful God must be to control all that!

KEY VERSE: *The heavens are telling the glory of God. They are a great display of what God can do. (Psalm 19:1)*

RELATED VERSES: *Joshua 10:13; 1 Kings 18:1ff.; 2 Kings 20:8-11; 2 Chronicles 7:12ff.; Psalm 19:1-6; 104:19; 148:3; Hebrews 1:2-3*

RELATED QUESTIONS: *How does God make the weather? Can God make the weather so that it'll be sunny tomorrow?*

NOTE TO PARENTS: *Part of this is a science issue. If your children are wondering how the forces of nature work, don't be afraid of encouraging them to learn more about the natural sciences. The power and wonder of nature can be used to inspire awe and worship of God. The heavens declare his glory! (See Psalm 19.)*

CREATION

ADAM
AND
EVE

Q: WHY DID GOD MAKE PEOPLE?

10

A: People are special creations, not just different animals. God created people to be his friends and to take care of the world. Unlike animals, human beings can talk to each other and to God. People are the only part of God's marvelous creation that can be friends with God. And he created them perfect—that's why Adam and Eve were not ashamed of their nakedness. But people are also the only ones who can sin.

KEY VERSES: *Then God said, "Let us make a man—someone like ourselves. He will be the master of all life upon the earth and in the skies and in the seas." So God made man like his Maker. Like God did God make man. Man and maid did he make them. (Genesis 1:26-27)*

RELATED VERSES: *Genesis 2:4-7; Psalm 8:4-5; 139:13-18*

RELATED QUESTIONS: *Why did God make people in addition to animals? Why did God make women?*

Q: HOW DID GOD MAKE ADAM AND EVE?

11

A: God made Adam and Eve, the first human beings, by using material that he had already made. God formed Adam just the way he wanted him to look and then brought Adam to life. God made Eve from part of Adam so that she would match him perfectly.

KEY VERSES: *The time came when the Lord God formed a man's body. He made it from the dust of the ground. Then he breathed into it the breath of life. And man became a living person. . . . Then the Lord God caused the man to fall into a deep sleep. He took one of the man's ribs. Then he closed up the place from which he had taken it. Then he made the rib into a woman, and brought her to the man. (Genesis 2:7, 21-22)*

RELATED VERSES: *Genesis 1:26–2:25; 3:19; 1 Timothy 2:13*

RELATED QUESTIONS: *Why did God make Eve from Adam's rib? Why did God make us out of dust?*

NOTE TO PARENTS: *A young child's concrete understanding can be a barrier to understanding this because the creation of Adam and Eve was a miracle. Explaining it as such may be the best approach, especially if your child is asking about the exact process that God used.*

Q: WHAT DID ADAM AND EVE "DRESS" THE LAND WITH?

12

A: The word *dress* that is used in some Bible versions means "take care of" or "tend." So when God told Adam and Eve to "dress" the land, he was telling them to take care of the rest of his creation.

KEY VERSE: *And the Lord God took the man, and put him into the garden of Eden to dress it and to keep it. (Genesis 2:15, KJV)*

RELATED VERSES: *Genesis 18:7; Deuteronomy 28:39; 2 Samuel 12:4*

NOTE TO PARENTS: *This kind of question is a good example of why it is important to choose an age-appropriate translation of the Bible for your child. There are many excellent translations from which to choose. The best one for your child is the one that uses words that he or she already knows.*

Q: HOW DID GOD MAKE EVERYONE ELSE AFTER ADAM AND EVE?

13

A: When God created animals and plants, he gave them the ability to reproduce themselves. The same is true with Adam and Eve—God created them with the ability to make babies. Adam and Eve had babies; then, when those children grew up, they got married and also had children. Those children also grew up and had babies. As time went on, there were more and more people on the earth. And although God didn't make each person the same way he created Adam and Eve, he was still involved with the creation of each one, watching over and putting him or her (and you) together just right.

KEY VERSE: *Then Adam lay with Eve his wife. She conceived and gave birth to a son, Cain (meaning "I have created"). For, as she said, "With God's help, I have created a man!" Her next child was his brother, Abel. Abel became a shepherd. Cain was a farmer. (Genesis 4:1-2)*

RELATED VERSES: *Genesis 1:28; 5:1-18; 6:1; Psalm 139: 13-18; Ezekiel 36:11; Hebrews 6:14*

RELATED QUESTIONS: *Did God make me the same way he made Adam? Did Eve have a belly button?*

NOTE TO PARENTS: *Many parents avoid this issue because they are uncomfortable talking about sex. Don't communicate nonverbally that this is a dirty or embarrassing topic. But at the same time, don't give children more information than they want or need.*

Q: HOW DID ADAM KNOW WHAT TO NAME THE ANIMALS?

14

A: God gave Adam the job of naming the animals, much like when your parents might ask you to name your pet. Adam named the animals whatever he wanted. But Adam didn't speak English, so the names he used are not the ones we use today. Adam lived a very long time ago, and today each language has its own words for the animals in our world.

KEY VERSES: *So the Lord God formed from the soil every kind of animal and bird. He brought them to the man to see what he would call them. Whatever the man called them, that was their name. (Genesis 2:19-20)*

RELATED VERSES: *Acts 13:2; Colossians 4:17*

Q: WHY DID ADAM AND EVE EAT THE FORBIDDEN FRUIT IF GOD SAID NOT TO?

15

A: Adam and Eve were sinless and perfect when God created them. But they still could choose to do what was wrong (just like you can choose to do what you aren't supposed to). When the devil tempted them to eat the forbidden fruit, they chose to do it. Although people talk about Adam and Eve eating an "apple" in the Garden of Eden, we don't know what the fruit looked like or how it tasted. All we know is that it was the one fruit in that big, beautiful garden that they weren't supposed to eat. Adam and Eve ate the fruit because the devil started them thinking about what it would be like. Then he lied about God's rule to make them think that God was keeping something good from them. Pretty soon they wanted to eat the fruit more than they wanted to obey God's rule.

KEY VERSES: *The serpent was the craftiest of all the creatures the Lord God had made. So the serpent came to the woman. "Really?" he asked. "None of the fruit in the garden? God says you mustn't eat any of it?" "Of course we may eat it," the woman told him. "It's only the fruit from the tree at the center of the garden that we must not eat. God says we must not eat it or even touch it. If we do, we will die." "That's a lie" the serpent hissed. "You'll not die! God knows very well that as soon as you eat it you will become like him. Your eyes will be opened. You will be able to know good from evil!" The woman was convinced. How lovely and fresh-looking it was! And it would make her so wise! So she ate some of the fruit and gave some to her husband. He ate it too. (Genesis 3:1-6)*

RELATED VERSES: *Matthew 6:13; 26:41*

ADAM AND EVE

Q: WHY DIDN'T ADAM DIE WHEN GOD SAID HE WOULD?

16

A: When Adam and Eve disobeyed God and ate the fruit, sin entered the world. That was the first sin ever! And when sin came into the world, death came with it. There are two kinds of death, and both came to Adam and Eve and to the world. First, there is physical death. Although Adam and Eve didn't die immediately when they took a bite of the fruit, eventually they *would* die. From that moment on, all plants, animals, and humans would die eventually. Second, there is spiritual death. That means being separated from God, being his enemies instead of his friends. This death came to Adam and Eve, and to all of us, the moment they disobeyed God. The only way to avoid this death forever is to trust in Christ. That's why Jesus came to earth—to die in our place, for our sin, so that we might have eternal life!

KEY VERSES: *When Adam sinned, sin entered the whole human race. His sin spread death through all the world. Everything began to grow old and die because all sinned. . . . For this one man, Adam, brought death to many through his sin. But this one man, Jesus Christ, brought forgiveness to many through God's mercy. Adam's one sin brought the penalty of death to many. But Christ freely takes away many sins and gives new life instead. (Romans 5:12, 15-16)*

RELATED VERSES: *Hebrews 9:27; James 4:14*

Q: DID GOD KNOW ADAM AND EVE WERE GOING TO SIN?

17

A: God knows everything, even before it happens, so he knew that Adam and Eve were going to sin. Still, God was very disappointed with what Adam and Eve did. But because God loved them (and because he loves us), he made a way for the sin to be forgiven. God's plan was to send Jesus to die on the cross for Adam's, Eve's, and our sins. By trusting in Christ, we can have eternal life.

KEY VERSES: *Long ago, before he made the world, God chose us to be his very own. He did this because of what Christ would do for us. He decided then to make us holy in his eyes, without a single fault. We stand before him covered with his love. His plan has always been to adopt us into his own family. He would do this by sending Jesus Christ to die for us. And he did this because he wanted to! (Ephesians 1:4-5)*

RELATED VERSES: *John 2:23-25; Acts 17:26-27*

NOTE TO PARENTS: *The knowledge that God knows everything can give your children a sense of security. Children can't do anything that will surprise God. He may be happy or disappointed, but he won't be surprised. Also, be aware that your children may not understand what the word penalty means. So be prepared to offer a simple explanation.*

Q: WHAT DOES GOD LOOK LIKE?

18

A: No one knows what God "looks like" because God is invisible and doesn't have a physical body as we do. But we can learn about God and see what God acts like by learning about his Son, Jesus. In the Bible we can read about how Jesus lived, how he treated people, and what he taught. That's what God is like.

KEY VERSE: *Jesus replied, "Don't you even yet know who I am, Philip? And I have been with you for all this time! Anyone who has seen me has seen the Father! So why are you asking to see him?" (John 14:9)*

RELATED VERSES: *John 1:18; 5:37; 6:46; 1 John 3:2*

RELATED QUESTIONS: *Does God have a beard? Is God bald?*

Q: DOES GOD HAVE FRIENDS OR IS HE ALONE?

19

A: God doesn't have other "gods" to be friends with. He is the only God there is. God doesn't need friends the way we do; he is perfectly happy being alone. But God also wants to have friendship with us. In fact, God wants to be our closest friend. So he has done a lot to make friends with us and to have our friendship. That's why he created us, sent Jesus to save us, gave us the Bible, and gave us the church.

KEY VERSES: *And you are my friends if you obey me. I no longer call you slaves. For a master doesn't confide in his slaves. Now you are my friends. This is proved by the fact that I have told you all that the Father told me. (John 15:14-15)*

RELATED VERSES: *Genesis 1:26; John 17:3*

RELATED QUESTIONS: *Are there other gods? Does God ever get lonely?*

Q: WHERE DOES GOD LIVE?

20

A: Sometimes we think of God as though he were another person like us. And just as we can only be one place at a time and we need a place to live, we think that God is the same way. But God isn't limited to a physical body or to one place at a time. In fact, God lives everywhere, especially inside people who love him. We call church "God's house" because that's where people who love God gather together to worship him. But no matter where we are, God is with us. We can never be lost to his love. God also lives in heaven— eventually, we will live there, too.

KEY VERSES: *[Solomon is speaking] "But is it possible that God would live on earth? Why, even the skies and the highest heavens cannot hold you! This Temple I have built will not be able to hold you either! And yet, O Lord my God, you have heard and answered what I asked. Please watch over this Temple night and day. For this is the place you have promised to live. Please listen to my prayers here, whether by night or by day. Listen to every prayer of the people of Israel. Listen to them when they face this place to pray. Yes, hear in heaven where you live. And when you hear, forgive." (1 Kings 8:27-30)*

RELATED VERSES: *Psalm 139:7-12; Acts 17:24-29; Romans 8:38-39; Ephesians 4:8-10*

RELATED QUESTIONS: *Does God live in the mountains? Where is heaven? How can God live in my heart? Does God live in church? How can God be everywhere? Is God a person or a ghost? How big is God?*

Q: DOES GOD SLEEP, OR DOES HE JUST REST?

21

A: God does not have a physical body like us, so he doesn't need to sleep or eat. When the Bible says God "rests," it means he has stopped doing something. To us, that is like rest. But God doesn't get tired or worn out, so he doesn't need to rest the way we do. And when we go to sleep at night, God doesn't close his eyes too—he continues to watch over us.

KEY VERSES: *He will never let me stumble, slip, or fall. For he is always watching, never sleeping. (Psalm 121:3-4)*

RELATED VERSES: *Genesis 2:2; 1 Kings 18:27; Ecclesiastes 8:16-17*

RELATED QUESTIONS: *Will I be safe at night? What does God do in heaven? Does God eat?*

NOTE TO PARENTS: *This kind of question arises from the faulty thinking that God is just like people. Most false gods that have been made up by various cultures, such as those the Canaanites worshiped or the Greek gods, were much like comic book superheros—just like people with superhuman abilities. But God isn't just a greater human. Clearing up this question will correct this faulty way of thinking about God.*

Q: WHO CREATED GOD?

22

A: No one created God—he has always existed. We can't understand this because everything that we know has a beginning or an end. Each day has a morning and night; basketball games have an opening tip-off and a final buzzer; people are born and they die. But God has no beginning or end. He always was and always will be.

KEY VERSES: *Lord, through all the generations you have been our home! You were there before the mountains were made. You were there before the earth was formed. You are God without beginning or end. (Psalm 90:1-2)*

RELATED VERSES: *Hebrews 13:8; Revelation 1:8, 18*

RELATED QUESTIONS: *Where did God come from? Will God ever die? How old is God?*

Q: WHY CAN'T WE SEE GOD?

23

A: We can't see God because he's invisible. But we *can* see what he does. Balloons are filled with air that we can't see, but we see the balloon get big as the air is put in. Radio waves are invisible, but they exist. Just because we can't see God doesn't mean he isn't real. Believing that God is there even though we can't see him is *faith*. Someday, in heaven, we will see God face to face.

KEY VERSE: *We can see and understand only a little about God now. It is like we were looking at his reflection in a poor mirror. Someday we are going to see him face to face. Now all that I know is hazy and blurred. But then I will see everything clearly. I will see as clearly as God sees into my heart right now. (1 Corinthians 13:12)*

RELATED VERSES: *John 1:18; Colossians 1:15; 1 Timothy 1:17; Hebrews 11:27*

RELATED QUESTION: *Why doesn't God let everyone see him so everyone will believe him?*

NOTE TO PARENTS: *Young children struggle with this because of their concrete way of thinking. Using illustrations like the ones here are helpful, but still imperfect; we can't see air because it's molecules don't form a solid enough image for us to see, not because it has no physical form. In contrast, God is invisible to us because he is a spirit.*

Q: CAN CHRISTIANS HEAR GOD TALKING TO THEM?

24

A: In the Bible we read about people hearing God's voice. Today, the main way that God speaks to us is through the Bible. That's why it's called "God's Word"—the Bible is God's message to us. God may also speak to us through people and circumstances and in other ways. But God will never tell us to do something that goes against what he says in the Bible. And don't forget, God is with us all the time.

KEY VERSES: *Long ago God spoke in many different ways to our fathers. He spoke through the prophets in visions, dreams, and even face to face. Little by little he told them about his plans. But now in these days he has spoken to us through his Son. He has given his Son everything. Through his Son he made the world and everything there is. (Hebrews 1:1-2)*

RELATED VERSES: *1 Samuel 3:1-18; Psalm 119:1-24*

RELATED QUESTIONS: *How can I hear God? Does my heart have ears?*

Q: DAD, WHY DO I NEED TWO FATHERS, YOU AND GOD?

25

A: We call God "our Father" because he created us, watches over us, and provides everything we need. He's like a human father, only perfect. God has given us human fathers and mothers to take care of us on earth. That's why God tells children to obey their parents and their heavenly Father—it's for their own good.

KEY VERSE: *[Jesus is speaking] "You sinful men even know how to give good gifts to your children. So won't your Father in Heaven be sure to give good gifts to those who ask him for them?" (Matthew 7:11)*

RELATED VERSES: *Exodus 20:12; Ephesians 6:1-3*

RELATED QUESTIONS: *What does it mean that God is our Father? What's the same and different about human fathers and God? Why does God say kids have to obey their parents?*

Q: DOES GOD SEE EVERYTHING THAT WE DO?

26

A:

Yes, God sees everything we do, both good and bad. We can't hide from him. God is happy when we do what is right and sad when we do wrong. God can reward us for doing what's right, even when no one else knows about it.

KEY VERSES: *[Elihu is speaking] "For God watches the deeds of all mankind. He sees them all. No darkness is thick enough to hide evil men from his eyes." (Job 34:21-22)*

RELATED VERSES: *Job 11:11; 31:4; Psalm 147:5; Matthew 10:28-31*

RELATED QUESTIONS: *Does God see the bad things I do? How can God know everything? How can God see everywhere?*

NOTE TO PARENTS: *This question may arise from a guilty conscience. Your child may want to talk about something that he or she did.*

JESUS

Q: IS JESUS GOD?

27

A: Jesus is fully God. When he came to earth and was born of the Virgin Mary, Jesus also became a human being, a person like you. So Jesus is both God and man. As God, Jesus has always existed—he was not created when he was born. Instead, he willingly chose to take on a human body.

KEY VERSES: *Before anything else existed, there was God's Son. He was the Word, and he was with God. He has always been alive and is himself God. (John 1:1-2)*

RELATED VERSES: *John 1:14; 14:9; Colossians 1:15-18*

RELATED QUESTION: *Did God create Jesus?*

Q: HOW CAN GOD BE THREE PERSONS AND ONE PERSON AT THE SAME TIME?

28

A: We don't know *how* God can be three persons at the same time, but we know he is because the Bible tells us so. The idea of three in one (the Trinity) is very hard to understand. Some people use the example of water. Water can be a liquid, a gas, or a solid. We usually see water in liquid form, as when we use it for drinking or for taking a bath. But water can also be a gas, as when it turns to steam. And it can be a solid, in the form of ice. But whether liquid, gas, or solid, it's still water. In some ways God is like a family with father, mother, and child—three persons and one family. Just remember that the Trinity does not mean that we have three gods. There is one God with three persons. The Trinity also does not mean that God wears three hats, or takes on three roles, at different times. All three persons—Father, Son, and Holy Spirit—have always existed.

KEY VERSE: *[Jesus is speaking] "So now go and make disciples in all the nations. Baptize them into the name of the Father, the Son, and the Holy Spirit." (Matthew 28:19)*

RELATED VERSES: *Matthew 3:16-17; John 14:7, 9-10*

RELATED QUESTION: *Why are there three people in the Trinity?*

Q: DO GOD AND JESUS CRY?

29

A: As a man, Jesus cried real tears when he was sad. God does not shed tears today, but he feels sad when people are hurting, when they disobey him, and when they don't believe in him. We can bring God joy by living as we should, showing love to others, and telling people about Christ.

KEY VERSE: *Tears came to Jesus' eyes. (John 11:35)*

RELATED VERSES: *Luke 19:41; John 11:33; Ephesians 4:30; Revelation 7:17*

RELATED QUESTION: *Does God have a heart?*

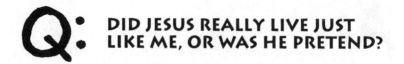

Q: DID JESUS REALLY LIVE JUST LIKE ME, OR WAS HE PRETEND?

30

A: Jesus is real. He came to earth and was born as a baby (we celebrate Jesus' birth at Christmas). And he lived like other ordinary people. Some stories we read and hear are made up and weren't meant to be taken as true. But the stories in the Bible really happened, and that's where we can read about Jesus.

KEY VERSE: *Christ was alive when the world began. I have seen him with my own eyes and listened to him speak. I have touched him with my own hands. He is God's message of life. (1 John 1:1)*

RELATED VERSES: *John 20:27; 1 Timothy 3:16; Hebrews 4:15*

Q: DID JESUS EVER DO ANYTHING BAD WHEN HE WAS LITTLE?

31

A: Jesus was born as a baby and grew up as a little boy and into a young man. When he was a child, Jesus had to learn many things, like how to hold a cup, how to talk, and how to count. He learned things from his parents and went to school to learn, too. But though Jesus was a real human being, he never did anything wrong—he never sinned—like stealing, lying, disobeying his parents, or saying bad words. Sometimes Jesus did things that *others* said were bad—like helping certain people and speaking out against wrong. But Jesus always did what was right—he always obeyed God.

KEY VERSES: *This suffering is all part of the work God has given you. Christ, who suffered for you, is your example. Follow in his steps. He never sinned. He never told a lie. He never answered back when insulted. When he suffered he did not threaten to get even. He left his case in the hands of God who always judges fairly. (1 Peter 2:21-23)*

RELATED VERSES: *Luke 2:41-51; Hebrews 5:9; 1 Peter 1:18-19*

RELATED QUESTIONS: *Did Jesus ever fight with his brothers? Did Jesus go to school?*

Q: IF JESUS DIED ON THE CROSS, HOW CAN HE BE ALIVE TODAY?

32

A: Jesus lived as a real human being. Jesus' death was a real death, too (he really died on the cross)—the people who killed him made sure of that. When Jesus was killed, all of his followers were very sad. Jesus' body was put in a grave. But three days later, God brought Jesus back to life. Jesus showed his wounds to his disciples. Jesus lives in his special "glorified" body in heaven today. Isn't that great?

KEY VERSES: *I passed on to you from the first what had been told to me. Christ died for our sins just as the Bible said he would. He was buried, and three days later he rose from the grave. This happened just as the prophets said it would. (1 Corinthians 15:3-4)*

RELATED VERSES: *John 20:27; 1 Corinthians 15:12-58*

RELATED QUESTIONS: *Did Jesus really die? Does Jesus still have scrapes and cuts on his body? How did Jesus rise from the dead? Is Jesus invisible now?*

NOTE TO PARENTS: *We call Jesus' postresurrection body a "glorified" body. Jesus was recognized by the disciples, and he ate a meal with them. But he also was able to appear suddenly in their midst—he wasn't limited by space and time. We really don't know anything more about what his body was like or what our body will be like. (See Luke 24:36-43 and John 20:19-31.)*

Q: WHY DO I FEEL AFRAID IF JESUS IS WITH ME?

33

A: Jesus is always with us even though we don't see him and often we don't feel any different. Jesus wants us to learn to trust him, to believe and know that he is there. It's natural to feel afraid. In fact, being afraid can be good. We should be afraid of danger. For example, fear can keep us a safe distance from a mean dog or something else that might hurt us. God wants our fears to remind us to trust him. Being afraid should be a signal to trust God and do what he wants us to do. But it doesn't mean that Jesus isn't with us.

KEY VERSE: *May the Lord of peace himself give you his peace no matter what happens. The Lord be with you all. (2 Thessalonians 3:16)*

RELATED VERSES: *Matthew 28:20; Philippians 4:6*

Q: HOW DID JESUS WALK ON WATER?

34

A: Jesus did a lot of miracles. We don't know how he did them. Jesus is God, so he can do anything. Walking on the water was not Jesus' ordinary way of getting around. He did this miracle, like other miracles, to teach his disciples and to show them his power. Jesus is Lord of the laws of the universe—he's in charge of the water, too, so he can walk on it whenever he wants to.

KEY VERSES: *That evening his disciples went down to the shore to wait for him. Darkness fell and Jesus still hadn't come back. So they got into the boat and headed out across the lake toward Capernaum. But soon a storm swept down upon them as they rowed. The sea grew very rough. And they were in the middle of the lake. Suddenly they saw Jesus walking toward the boat! They were terrified. So he called out to them and told them not to be afraid. Then they were willing to let him come to them. And suddenly the boat was already at the place where they were going! (John 6:16-21)*

RELATED VERSES: *Matthew 14:23-32; Mark 4:35-41; 6:45-51*

NOTE TO PARENTS: *Lots of well-meaning people have tried to explain miracles (such as Jesus' walking on the water) to make them believable to children. But this is a tragic mistake. The fact that miracles are incredible is exactly the point—they show us that God is awesome and powerful.*

Q: WHY DID JESUS DRESS SO FUNNY?

35

A: The clothes worn by Jesus and his followers may look different to us today, but they were in style back then. Jesus wore what people wore at that time. His clothes fit the climate and culture of the day. No one who lived in Jesus' time told him that he dressed funny, and they should know.

KEY VERSES: *So the soldiers crucified Jesus. Then they put his clothes into four piles. There was one piece of clothing for each of them. But they said, "Let's not tear up his robe," for it was seamless. "Let's throw dice to see who gets it." This fulfilled the Scriptures. It said, "They divided my clothes among them and cast lots for my robe." (John 19:23-24)*

RELATED VERSES: *Psalm 22:18; Matthew 27:35*

NOTE TO PARENTS: *Children get their idea of how Jesus dressed from Bible and Sunday school art. This is what we think Jesus might have looked like, but we have no pictures or descriptions of his physical appearance, so we don't know exactly what he looked like.*

Q: WHY DID THEY BEAT UP JESUS?

36

A: Some people got very angry at Jesus because he was speaking against the bad things they were doing. They tried to get Jesus to do what they wanted. Instead, Jesus did what God wanted him to do, and he told everybody how bad those people were. Finally the people got so angry at Jesus that they wanted to kill him. And eventually, that's what they did.

KEY VERSES: *Then the Roman soldiers took him into the barracks of the palace. They called out the whole palace guard. They dressed him in a purple robe. And they made a crown of sharp thorns and put it on his head. Then they cheered, yelling, "Yea! King of the Jews!" They beat him on the head with a cane and spat on him. They made fun of him by bowing down to "worship" him. (Mark 15:16-19)*

RELATED VERSES: *Isaiah 53:4-10; Matthew 26:57-68; Mark 15:15; John 15:14-18*

RELATED QUESTIONS: *Why did they put a thorny crown on Jesus? If Jesus was such a good man, why were people mad at him?*

Q: WHY DID GOD LET THEM HURT JESUS?

37

A: When Jesus was being hurt, he could have called on angels to save him. After all, he was God's Son. But Jesus chose to suffer and die *for us*. Jesus loved us so much that he did what it took to pay for our sins. Jesus and the Father agreed that it was necessary for him to die on the cross.

KEY VERSES: *He has so much kindness! He took away all our sins through the blood of his Son. This saved us. He has showered upon us the richness of his grace. He understands us and knows what is best for us at all times. God has told us his secret reason for sending Christ. He has a plan he decided on in mercy long ago. He plans to gather us all together when the time is ripe. He will gather his people in Heaven and on earth. They will be with him in Christ forever. (Ephesians 1:7-10)*

RELATED VERSES: *Matthew 26:53; 27:46; 1 John 2:2*

RELATED QUESTION: *Why didn't Jesus save himself from dying on the cross?*

Q: WHY DO THEY CALL IT GOOD FRIDAY IF THAT'S THE DAY JESUS DIED?

38

A: The day Jesus died is called "Good Friday"
because it was a good day for us—Jesus died
for us, in our place. That day was both a happy day and
a sad day. It was sad because Jesus suffered and died. But
it was happy because Jesus paid the penalty for our sins.
At the time, the day was not seen as Good Friday. But by
Easter morning, after Jesus had been raised from the
dead, everybody knew it was good.

KEY VERSES: *He was taken out of the city. He carried his
cross to the place known as "The Skull." In Hebrew it
was called "Golgotha." There they crucified him and two
others with him. One was on either side, with Jesus
between them. (John 19:17-18)*

RELATED VERSES: *Matthew 27:32–28:20; Mark 15:16-47;
Luke 23:26-56*

Q: WHY DOES JESUS WANT US TO FOLLOW HIM?

39

A: Jesus told the people to follow him because he is the way to God, heaven, and eternal life. When Jesus was on earth, the disciples and others followed him by walking close to him and listening to his words. Today, we follow Jesus by copying his example and by doing what he says.

KEY VERSES: *Then Jesus said to the disciples, "Do you want to be my followers? If you do, you must deny yourselves. You must take up your cross and follow me. For anyone who keeps his life for himself shall lose it. And anyone who loses his life for me shall find it again. What good is it if you gain the whole world and lose eternal life? What could ever be as good as eternal life?" (Matthew 16:24-26)*

RELATED VERSES: *Matthew 4:19; John 14:6*

Q: WHY DID JESUS GET TEMPTED BY THE DEVIL?

40

A: When someone tempts you, that person is trying to get you to do something. Because Satan is against Jesus, he tried to get Jesus to do something wrong, to sin. But Jesus didn't give in—he didn't sin. Being tempted isn't sin; giving in to temptation is.

KEY VERSES: *This High Priest of ours understands how weak we are. He had the same temptations we do. But he never once gave way to them and sinned. So let us come boldly to the throne of God. There he will give us his mercy. And there we will find grace to help in times of need. (Hebrews 4:15-16)*

RELATED VERSES: *Matthew 4:1-11; Mark 1:12-13; Luke 4:1-13*

RELATED QUESTION: *What does "being tempted" mean?*

Q: WHY DIDN'T GOD JUST FORGIVE EVERYBODY?

41

A: It would not be right or fair for God to just forgive everyone. There is a penalty that must be paid for doing wrong. The penalty for sinning against God is death, eternal death. But God loved us so much that he sent Jesus, his only Son, to pay our penalty. Jesus did this by dying on the cross, in our place. Now everyone can be forgiven by trusting in Christ.

KEY VERSES: *Yes, all have sinned. All fall short of God's perfect glory. But if we trust in Jesus Christ, God says we are "not guilty." In his kindness he freely takes away our sins. God sent Christ Jesus to take the punishment for our sins. He ended all God's anger against us. Christ's blood and our faith saves us from God's anger. This is the way he could be fair to everybody. He did not punish the people who sinned before Christ came. He was looking forward to the time when Christ would come and take away those sins. (Romans 3:23-25)*

RELATED VERSES: *Mark 8:31; John 3:16; Romans 5:8; Hebrews 2:14-17; 8:3; 9:13-14, 22-23; 1 John 1:7*

RELATED QUESTION: *Why did Jesus have to die?*

SALVATION

Q: WHY DO GOD AND JESUS LOVE PEOPLE?

42

A: God loves us because that's what he decided to do. God doesn't love us because we're good or nice people. In fact, no one could ever be good enough to be worthy of God's love. Isn't it amazing that God loves us even though we sometimes ignore him and disobey him?

KEY VERSE: *But God showed his great love for us. He sent Christ to die for us while we were still sinners. (Romans 5:8)*

RELATED VERSES: *John 1:12; 16:7*

NOTE TO PARENTS: *The best way to help children understand God's love is to demonstrate it to them. Hug them, train them, cheer them, guide them, discipline them, talk to them, spend time with them, accept them, forgive them, help them, stand by them, and provide for them— then they'll understand.*

Q: HOW CAN JESUS FIT IN MY HEART?

43

A: When we say "heart," we mean deep down inside us—where we really feel and believe. So when someone says, "Jesus lives in my heart," the person means that he has asked Jesus to be his Savior— to forgive and take care of him—and that Jesus is in charge of his life. When someone asks Jesus to take over, God really does come inside—the Holy Spirit comes and lives inside that person. And the Holy Spirit can be in all of the people who love God at the same time. Jesus wants to be very close to you, too, like a good friend. Through his Holy Spirit, he wants to "live in your heart."

KEY VERSES: *He has kept this secret for centuries and generations past. But now he is pleased to tell it to the brothers and sisters. The riches and glory of his plan are for you Gentiles, too. This is the secret: Christ in your hearts is your only hope of glory. (Colossians 1:26-27)*

RELATED VERSES: *John 16:7-8; Acts 1:8; 1 Thessalonians 4:8*

RELATED QUESTION: *How can other people have Jesus in their hearts if he's in mine?*

NOTE TO PARENTS: *Children are often told that Jesus comes to live inside their hearts when they believe in him. Young children take this literally and think that a miniaturized Jesus actually lives in their chest. "Jesus lives in my heart" is a shorthand way of calling Jesus Savior and Lord. "Jesus goes with you everywhere" may be a better way of phrasing it for young children.*

Q: HOW DO YOU GET JESUS IN YOUR HEART?

44

A: You become a Christian by asking Jesus to take over your life. You know that you have done wrong things, that you have sinned, and you recognize that you need Jesus to forgive your sins. So you tell Jesus about your sins and that you are sorry, and you ask for his forgiveness. Then you do what Jesus says.

KEY VERSES: *But now God has shown us another way to Heaven. It is not by "being good enough" and trying to keep his laws. It is by a new way. It is not really new. Because the Scriptures told about it long ago. Now God says he will accept us and declare us "not guilty." He will do this if we trust Jesus Christ to take away our sins. We all can be saved by coming to Christ. It doesn't matter who we are or what we have been like. Yes, all have sinned. All fall short of God's perfect glory. But if we trust in Jesus Christ, God says we are "not guilty." In his kindness he freely takes away our sins. (Romans 3:21-24)*

RELATED VERSES: *John 5:24; Acts 19:18; 1 John 1:9*

RELATED QUESTION: *How does someone become a Christian?*

Q: WOULD GOD SEND NICE PEOPLE TO HELL IF THEY ARE NOT CHRISTIANS?

45

A: Compared to each other, some people are nice and some are mean. But compared to God, all people are not very good. All people need to be forgiven for their sins, not just "mean people." To be fair, God has to punish sin. God doesn't *want* to send anyone to hell. That's why he sent Jesus—to pay the penalty for our sins by dying on the cross. But, unfortunately, not all people are willing to admit that they sin and ask for forgiveness. They don't accept the payment of Jesus' death for them. So God lets them experience the results of their choice.

KEY VERSES: *The Bible says, "No one is good without God. Every person in the world has sinned." No one has ever really followed God's paths or even truly wanted to. Everyone has turned away from God. All have gone wrong. No one anywhere has kept on doing what is right. (Romans 3:10-12)*

RELATED VERSES: *Romans 5:16; Jude 1:4*

RELATED QUESTION: *Who will God send to hell?*

Q: IF I SWEAR, WILL I GO TO HELL WHEN I DIE?

46

A: Although it is very important to watch what we say, God doesn't decide who goes to hell because of our speech. Instead, our forgiveness and eternal life are based on the death and resurrection of Jesus Christ. If we trust Jesus to save us, we are forgiven. Of course that doesn't make it all right to swear. We should always try to speak and do what is right.

KEY VERSES: *Because of his kindness, you have been saved through trusting Christ. And even that trust is not your own. It, too, is a gift from God. Salvation is not a reward for the good we have done. So none of us can take any credit for it. (Ephesians 2:8-9)*

RELATED VERSES: *Romans 3:14; James 3:10*

RELATED QUESTION: *What happens to people who use bad words?*

NOTE TO PARENTS: *Many children think they are too bad or evil to be forgiven by God. If you sense that your child feels this way, he or she needs to know that God can forgive any sin. Tell your children that they are not uniquely bad—all people sin.*

Q: WILL ALL OF MY FRIENDS GO TO HEAVEN?

47

A: God loves your friends just as he loves you. Only God knows who will go to heaven and hell; we don't. But there is only one way to heaven—through Jesus. So we can go to heaven only if we have given our life to Christ. If your friends don't follow Jesus, you can help them understand by telling them the Good News about Jesus and how he died for them. Heaven is worth going to even if your friends don't. There will be no good times in hell.

KEY VERSE: *Jesus said, "I am the Way, the Truth, and the Life. No one can get to the Father except through me." (John 14:6)*

RELATED VERSES: *John 5:24; 11:25; Acts 4:12; 1 John 2:23*

RELATED QUESTION: *Does God love my friends?*

NOTE TO PARENTS: *This may be a good opportunity to encourage your child to invite a friend to church or Sunday school.*

Q: WHY ISN'T EVERYONE A CHRISTIAN?

48

A: Not everyone wants to be a Christian, and God doesn't force people to follow Jesus. Some people don't just reject Christ, they also act mean to Christians. That's because they don't understand the love that God has for them. We should try to tell these people about God's love for them.

KEY VERSES: *[Jesus is praying] "And now I am coming to you. I have told them many things while I was with them. They should be filled with my joy. I have given them your commands. And the world hates them. This is because they don't belong in the world, just as I don't. I'm not asking you to take them out of the world. I am asking that you keep them from the evil one. They are not part of this world any more than I am." (John 17:13-16)*

RELATED VERSES: *Matthew 7:14; John 15:9*

RELATED QUESTION: *Why do some people laugh when I talk about Jesus?*

NOTE TO PARENTS: *You can pray with your child for others to become Christians.*

Q: WHY DOESN'T GOD JUST ZAP THE BAD PEOPLE?

49

A: God loves people so much, even the worst people in the world, that he is giving them time to turn away from being bad and to turn to him. God is very patient. Someday, however, the time will be up, and all those who refuse to live God's way and give their lives to Christ will be punished. That will be a very sad day, but it will come.

KEY VERSE: *It may seem like he is slow in coming back as he promised. But he isn't. He is waiting because he does not want anyone to die. He is giving more time for sinners to repent. (2 Peter 3:9)*

RELATED VERSES: *Matthew 13:24-30; Hebrews 10:23*

RELATED QUESTION: *Why do people get away with being bad?*

Q: HOW LONG IS ETERNITY?

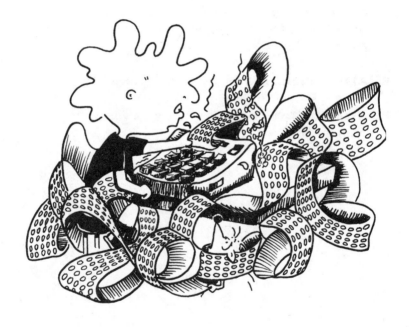

50

A: We can't even imagine how long eternity is. Eternity goes on forever. Sometimes we have good times that we wish would never end—such as a party or a vacation or a visit by a friend from out of town. But they do come to an end. Eternity, however, never ends. God is eternal, and he has given us eternal life. If we know Jesus, we will live forever with him, someday in heaven, after our life on earth comes to an end.

KEY VERSE: *But don't forget this, dear friends! A day is like 1,000 years to the Lord. (2 Peter 3:8)*

RELATED VERSES: *Psalm 41:13; 90:4; 1 Timothy 1:17*

RELATED QUESTION: *What is eternity?*

Q: WHAT DOES GOD WANT US TO DO?

51

A: In the Bible, God's Word, God tells us what he wants us to do, how he wants us to live. Although there are a lot of messages and information in the Bible, God's four main instructions for our lives are: (1) believe in Jesus and trust him every day; (2) obey Jesus and do what he says; (3) love God and others; (4) be fair and honest and live for God without being proud about it.

KEY VERSES: *They replied, "What should we do to satisfy God?" Jesus told them, "God's will is that you believe in the one he has sent." (John 6:28-29)*

RELATED VERSES: *Ecclesiastes 12:13-14; Micah 6:6-8; Matthew 19:19; 22:39*

RELATED QUESTION: *How can I know what God wants me to do?*

PRAYER

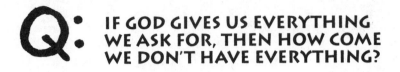

Q: IF GOD GIVES US EVERYTHING WE ASK FOR, THEN HOW COME WE DON'T HAVE EVERYTHING?

52

A: God doesn't give us everything we *ask* for. He gives us everything we *need*, when we need it. Sometimes we want things that could hurt us, such as when a baby wants to play in the fire. God knows what can hurt us, so he doesn't give us those things because he loves us. God wants to give us what is good for us.

KEY VERSE: *When you do ask you don't get it because your whole aim is wrong. You want only what will make you happy. (James 4:3)*

RELATED VERSES: *Matthew 7:7-11; 21:22; Luke 11:9*

RELATED QUESTION: *Why didn't I get what I prayed for?*

NOTE TO PARENTS: *If your child is older, you may want to explain that there are three types of pray-ers: (1) those who don't ask, (2) those who ask with the wrong motives, and (3) those who consider what God wants and pray accordingly. This question may be a chance to find a need that your child has and pray with him or her about it.*

Q: WHY DO WE PRAY?

53

A: Prayer is talking with God. When we have a good friend, we talk to that person about all sorts of things. That's part of being a friend. In the same way, we should talk to God about what is happening in our life. God wants us to share our life with him, to tell him about what makes us happy, sad, and afraid. He wants to know what we want and what we would like him to do, for ourself and for others. Also, when we pray, we open ourself up to God so that he can make good changes in us.

KEY VERSES: *Don't worry about anything. Instead, pray about everything. Tell God your needs, and don't forget to thank him for his answers. If you do this, you will find God's peace. It is far more wonderful than the human mind can understand. God's peace will keep your thoughts and your hearts as you trust in Christ Jesus. (Philippians 4:6-7)*

RELATED VERSES: *Luke 6:12; Acts 6:1-4; Ephesians 6:12-13; James 4:2*

RELATED QUESTION: *What is prayer?*

NOTE TO PARENTS: Practical Christianity *(LaVonne Neff and others, Tyndale House Publishers) and* What Is Prayer? *(Carolyn Nystrom, Moody Press) are two good resources for more on the topic of prayer.*

Q: WILL GOD GIVE CHILDREN TOYS IF THEY ASK HIM FOR THEM?

54

A: Some people think God is there to give us toys and other things we want. But God doesn't just hand out stuff to us. His purpose is to make us into people who are like Christ. God really cares about us, and he knows what we need. Although toys seem important sometimes, there are other things that we need more. God also doesn't want us to get our happiness from toys, but from him and from other people.

KEY VERSES: *You want what you don't have. So you kill to get it! You long for what others have. So you start a fight to take it away! Why don't you have what you want? Because you don't ask God for it. When you do ask you don't get it because your whole aim is wrong. You want only what will make you happy. (James 4:2-3)*

RELATED VERSES: *Philippians 4:4-10; 1 Thessalonians 5:17*

RELATED QUESTIONS: *If I pray for something, will God give it to me? Does God care about me?*

Q: WHAT SHOULD I SAY TO GOD WHEN I PRAY?

55

A: When we pray, it's easy to say the same words over and over. Prayer can become a habit that we don't think about. Instead, we should think about what we are saying when we pray, and we should be honest with God. Also, we shouldn't pray to show off, but we should say to God what we want to tell him. The Lord's Prayer can be a guide for what to talk to God about. Prayers can include thanking God for who he is and for what he has done. In prayer we can confess our sins, telling God that we are sorry for the bad things we have done. We can make requests, too, asking God to help others and to give us strength and guidance. We can talk to God about anything on our mind.

KEY VERSES: *[Jesus is speaking] "Pray like this: 'Our Father in Heaven, we honor your holy name. We ask that your kingdom will come now. May your will be done here on earth, just as it is in Heaven. Give us our food again today, as usual. And forgive us our sins, just as we have forgiven those who have sinned against us. Don't bring us into temptation. But keep us safe from the Evil One. Amen.'" (Matthew 6:9-13)*

RELATED VERSES: *Luke 11:1-13; Philippians 4:6; 1 Thessalonians 5:17; 1 Timothy 2:8; James 5:16*

NOTE TO PARENTS: *Children can get caught into a routine prayer. Look for ways to vary the family prayers in which your children participate. For example, you could suggest that each member of the family pray about what happened during the day, or you could compile a family prayer list and use it to guide your family prayer times.*

Q: HOW COME WHEN I PRAY TO GOD HE DOESN'T ALWAYS ANSWER?

Hello–you've reached heaven's 1-800 number. There isn't anyone here to take your call right now, but if you leave a long message at the sound of the choir, we will return your call. This is a recording...

56

A: There's a difference between hearing and answering. God hears all our prayers, but he doesn't always give us what we ask for. Also, he answers all our prayers, but not always the way we want him to. When we ask God for something, sometimes he answers no or wait. A good answer is not always yes.

KEY VERSES: *Yes, the Lord hears the good man when he calls for help. He saves him out of all his troubles. The Lord is close to those whose hearts are breaking. He saves those who are sorry for their sins. The good man does not escape all troubles. But the Lord helps him in each and every one. (Psalm 34:17-19)*

RELATED VERSES: *Psalm 139:4; 2 Corinthians 12:8; 1 Peter 5:7*

RELATED QUESTION: *Does God always hear my prayers?*

Q: WHY DID I HAVE A BAD DREAM WHEN I PRAYED BEFORE I WENT TO SLEEP?

57

A: It's good to pray before falling asleep at night. Praying helps us think through the day and thank God for how much he loves us. We should also pray for the next day. Christians aren't promised that they will be free from all problems and difficulties. God does promise to be with us during hard times. A lot of things can cause bad dreams—something on our mind, something we ate, a noise. Ask God to help you sleep, but remember that whatever happens, he is there with you.

KEY VERSE: *Then I lay down and slept in peace and woke up safely. For the Lord was watching over me. (Psalm 3:5)*

RELATED VERSES: *Psalm 34:17-19; 139:7-11; Proverbs 3:24-26; Matthew 2:12-13; Acts 2:17*

RELATED QUESTION: *If God is with me, why did he let me have a bad dream?*

Q: HOW CAN GOD HEAR EVERYONE'S PRAYERS AT ONCE?

58

A: God can hear everyone's prayers at once because God is everywhere. We can only be in one place at a time, and usually we can't understand more than one person at a time. But God is not like us—he is not limited. Not only can God hear and understand everyone who is praying to him in many different languages, but he also can give each person his full attention. Isn't that great?

KEY VERSES: *[God is speaking] "Am I a God who is only in one place? Do they think I cannot see what they are doing? Can anyone hide from me? Am I not everywhere in Heaven and earth at the same time?" (Jeremiah 23:23-24)*

RELATED VERSES: *Luke 1:13; Acts 10:31*

RELATED QUESTION: *How can God hear people praying at the same time from different countries?*

NOTE TO PARENTS: *Many children harbor the misconception that God is limited as we are. This is partly unavoidable because children think concretely. But it is also an opportunity for you to introduce them to the idea that God is infinitely greater than we are. He can even hear thousands of prayers at once! An illustration that might help: When five people touch you, you can feel all five.*

HEAVEN

AND

HELL

Q: IF WE WENT HIGH ENOUGH IN THE SKY, WOULD WE FIND HEAVEN?

59

A: No one but God knows exactly where heaven is. But the best way we can describe its location is to say it is "up." If we rode a spaceship up, way out into space, we would not find heaven—it can't be seen or found by people. Only God can take us there. And that's what he does, after we die, if we have trusted in Jesus as our Savior.

KEY VERSES: *Not long after this, Jesus rose into the sky. He went up into a cloud, leaving them staring after him. They were straining their eyes for another look at him. But suddenly two white-robed men were standing there with them. They said, "Men of Galilee, why are you standing here staring at the sky? Jesus has gone to Heaven. And someday he will come back again, just as he went!" (Acts 1:9-11)*

RELATED VERSES: *John 3:13; Luke 24:50-51*

RELATED QUESTIONS: *Where is heaven? Is heaven up?*

Q: WHAT IS HEAVEN LIKE?

60

A: The Bible uses some wonderful pictures to tell us what heaven is like. In our world, we think that gold is important because it's so valuable. But in heaven, the streets will be gold—we'll *walk* on it. The best way to picture heaven is to imagine the most exciting and fun place that you've ever been to. Heaven will be like that only much, much better. Jesus told his followers that he was leaving earth to go to heaven to prepare a place for them. He has a special place for us, where there is no crying or sadness and we will be filled with joy.

KEY VERSES: *[Jesus is speaking] "There are many homes in my Father's house. I am going to prepare a place for you. I will come again and take you to me. Then you will be with me where I am about to go. If this weren't so, I would tell you plainly." (John 14:2-3)*

RELATED VERSES: *Isaiah 60:17; Revelation 21:21*

RELATED QUESTIONS: *What will we do in heaven? Are the streets in heaven real gold or just painted gold?*

Q: IS THERE A MCDONALD'S IN HEAVEN?

61

A: No. In heaven, we won't need people to work to make us food. Our bodies will be different. They will be "glorified," or perfect, bodies. We don't know if we will eat there or what kind of food we will need. God will make sure that we have everything we need. Heaven will be fun. It will be great!

KEY VERSES: *[When Jesus appeared to the disciples] Still they stood there, unsure. They were filled with joy and doubt. Then he asked them, "Do you have anything here to eat?" They gave him a piece of broiled fish. And he ate it as they watched! (Luke 24:41-43)*

RELATED VERSES: *Romans 16:18; Philippians 3:19*

RELATED QUESTIONS: *What do we eat in heaven? Are there going to be things I enjoy in heaven? Is there school in heaven?*

NOTE TO PARENTS: *Children are concerned about food. Food is important to them, and they don't want to be hungry. Curiosity about what they will be eating in heaven may underlie questions like these.*

Q: WILL THERE BE TOYS IN HEAVEN?

62

A: We like toys because we have such fun with them. But we can get tired of toys, too. For example, you don't play with your baby toys any more. That's because you outgrew them and got tired of them. God will have just the right kind of toys for you in heaven. You will enjoy heaven even more than your favorite toys.

KEY VERSES: *When I was a child I thought like a child does. When I became a man I put away the childish things. We can see and understand only a little about God now. It is like we were looking at his reflection in a poor mirror. Someday we are going to see him face to face. Now all that I know is hazy and blurred. But then I will see everything clearly. I will see as clearly as God sees into my heart right now. (1 Corinthians 13:11-12)*

RELATED VERSES: *Ephesians 4:14; 1 Corinthians 14:20*

RELATED QUESTIONS: *Will I have my teddy bear in heaven? Do toys go to heaven?*

Q: WILL MY PET GO TO HEAVEN WHEN IT DIES?

63

A: We don't know what happens to animals when they die, but God does, and we know his plan is good. Sometimes we may get the idea that animals think and understand as we do. But God created animals different from people. Animals don't have souls or think as we do, so they can't enjoy God the way we can. Here on earth, pets are fun to play with and animals are interesting to watch. Only God knows if pets will join us in heaven.

KEY VERSES: *God made all sorts of wild animals and cattle and reptiles. And God was pleased with what he had done. Then God said, "Let us make a man—someone like ourselves. He will be the master of all life upon the earth and in the skies and in the seas." So God made man like his Maker. Like God did God make man. Man and maid did he make them. (Genesis 1:25-27)*

RELATED VERSES: *Isaiah 11:6-8; 65:25*

RELATED QUESTION: *Where do animals go when they die?*

NOTE TO PARENTS: *This question may be a way of testing the reality of heaven. A child's world is tied to his or her pet, and the death of a pet naturally raises the question of what happens to it afterward. But if you're not sure how to answer, don't be afraid of saying you don't know. The answer may not be as important as helping your child deal with losing a pet. When we get to heaven, God will give us everything we need to be filled with unspeakable joy.*

Q: WHY CAN'T WE GO TO HEAVEN AND JUST SEE IT AND THEN COME BACK?

64

A: This question is like asking, "Can I become a teenager and then come back to my age right now?" It's impossible because you have to *grow* into your teens; you can't simply jump there and back. In the same way, heaven is more than a place you can visit. It's a time at the end of life, and God has to make us ready to go there. In fact, we have to change in order to go there. We know that heaven exists because God has told us so in his Word, the Bible. And Jesus promised to "prepare a place" so that we can live with him forever (John 14:2). Once we get there, we won't want to come back.

KEY VERSES: *Then I looked and saw a door standing open in Heaven. I heard the same voice I had heard before. It was the one that sounded like a mighty trumpet blast. It said, "Come up! I will show you what must happen in the future!" And instantly I was in the spirit. And I saw a throne and someone sitting on it! Great bursts of light flashed forth from him. It was like light from a glittering diamond or from a shining ruby. There was a rainbow glowing like an emerald around his throne. (Revelation 4:1-3)*

RELATED VERSES: *Exodus 33:22; Matthew 17:2; 2 Corinthians 12:2-3*

RELATED QUESTIONS: *Is heaven really there? Why can't I go to heaven now? How do we get to heaven after we die?*

Q: WILL I HAVE MY SAME NAME IN HEAVEN?

65

A: When we get to heaven, we will see our friends and family members who have died and gone there before us. They will recognize us, and we will know them. The Bible says that when we trust Christ as Savior, our names are written in the "Book of Life." That's God's list of who gets into heaven.

KEY VERSE: *[Jesus is speaking] "All who conquer will be dressed in white. I will not erase their names from the Book of Life. I will announce before my Father and his angels that they are mine." (Revelation 3:5)*

RELATED VERSES: *Isaiah 62:1-3; Luke 16:19-24*

RELATED QUESTIONS: *Will people know me in heaven? Will I remember my family and friends in heaven? Will life in heaven be like it is here? Will I stay the same in heaven as I am here?*

Q: WILL GOD LET ME VISIT GRANDPA IN HEAVEN?

66

A: One of the great things about going to heaven is getting to see the people we love and want to see. If those people have trusted in Christ, they will be there. If your grandpa is in heaven, you will be able to see him when you go there.

KEY VERSES: *The believers who are dead will be the first to rise to meet the Lord. Then we who are alive and remain on the earth will be caught up with them. We will go to the clouds to meet the Lord in the air. We will stay with him forever. So comfort and cheer each other with this news. (1 Thessalonians 4:16-18)*

RELATED VERSES: *Daniel 7:13; Matthew 17:1-3; Acts 7:56*

RELATED QUESTION: *Why did God take Grandpa to heaven?*

NOTE TO PARENTS: *If a grandparent has died recently, your child will have many questions like this one. He or she may also want to express grief over the loss. Be open to talk to your child about his or her feelings.*

Q: WHY IS HELL DARK IF THEY HAVE FIRES?

67

A: The Bible uses a lot of pictures to give us an idea of what heaven and hell are like. Fire means burning and pain. Do you remember having a fever? You felt like you were burning up, but there was no flame. Darkness means loneliness. Can you imagine anything more lonely than sitting by yourself in total darkness? What God is telling us is that hell is a terrible place. We certainly don't want to go there.

KEY VERSE: *[Jesus is speaking] "And many . . . shall be thrown into outer darkness. They will be put in the place of crying and pain." (Matthew 8:12)*

RELATED VERSES: *Luke 16:28; Revelation 20:15*

RELATED QUESTIONS: *What's really happening in hell? What is hell like?*

NOTE TO PARENTS: *Children hear conflicting descriptions of hell. They hear that hell is a dark place (Matthew 8:12) and yet a lake of fire (Revelation 19:20). (They may also have heard that it is cold.) Instead of grasping the meanings of these metaphors, the child is taking the images concretely.*

Q: WHO ENDS UP IN HELL?

68

A: Hell is the place where God will punish Satan and his followers—and all those who refuse to follow God. We don't know exactly who will go there because we don't make that judgment, God does. But God has made it possible for everyone to escape punishment in hell. He gives everyone the opportunity to go to heaven. That's why he sent Jesus to die on the cross. When Jesus suffered and died, he took our place—he paid the penalty for our sins. So if we trust in Jesus, we can escape hell and go to heaven. It sure would be great if all our friends, family, and neighbors would end up in heaven. Let's tell them how to get there.

KEY VERSE: *Anyone whose name wasn't in the Book of Life was thrown into the Lake of Fire. (Revelation 20:15)*

RELATED VERSES: *John 3:16-18; 1 John 1:9*

RELATED QUESTIONS: *Are there kids in hell? Who goes to hell? Will I go to hell if I swear?*

ANGELS

AND

DEMONS

Q: WHAT DO ANGELS REALLY LOOK LIKE?

69

A: The word *angel* means "messenger." Angels are God's messengers. They can also be God's warriors. In the Bible we read about people who saw angels. Sometimes the people knew they were angels, and sometimes they didn't. Some angels described in the Bible have wings. Those angels are called cherubim. But most of the angels in the Bible stories looked like regular people. We don't know what angels look like in heaven.

KEY VERSES: *I, John, saw and heard all these things. I fell down to worship the angel who showed them to me. But he said, "No, don't do anything like that. I am a servant of Jesus like you, and like your brothers the prophets. I am like all those who hear and act on the truth stated in this book. Only worship God." (Revelation 22:8-9)*

RELATED VERSES: *Genesis 19:1; Hebrews 13:2*

RELATED QUESTIONS: *Are angels boys or girls? Do angels eat?*

NOTE TO PARENTS: *You may want to ask if your child has seen a picture of an angel, perhaps in a children's Bible, in a painting, in the cartoons, etc. Those pictures often leave mental impressions about an angel's appearance.*

Q: WHEN I DIE, WILL I BECOME AN ANGEL?

70

A: Angels are spiritual beings created by God. They are different from human beings. You are a spiritual being, too. In other words, you have a soul and will live forever and can know God. But you are also a physical being. You live on earth and have a physical body. When you die, you will leave your physical body behind and will be given a glorified or perfect body in heaven. We don't know exactly what our glorified bodies will be like, but we know that people in heaven will be able to recognize us. One thing is for sure, we don't become angels when we die. In fact, angels will serve us in heaven. Wow!

KEY VERSE: *Don't you know that we will judge the angels in Heaven? You should be able to decide your problems here on earth easily enough. (1 Corinthians 6:3)*

RELATED VERSES: *Psalm 8:5; Hebrews 2:7*

RELATED QUESTIONS: *How many angels are there? Do you have to die to be a spirit?*

NOTE TO PARENTS: *According to Matthew 26:53 and other passages, there are thousands of angels.*

Q: WHAT DOES MY ANGEL DO?

ROLLER COASTER MADNESS

71

A: Angels are God's helpers. They live in heaven with him. God often instructs angels to protect people by blocking the evil that Satan directs at them. Angels also carry out God's purposes in people's lives. In other words, angels help us do what God wants us to do.

KEY VERSE: *[Jesus is speaking] "Be careful that you don't look down upon a single one of these children. For I tell you that in Heaven their angels can speak directly to my Father." (Matthew 18:10)*

RELATED VERSES: *Genesis 24:7; Numbers 22:15-35; Daniel 3:28; 6:22; Matthew 1:21-24; 4:11; Hebrews 1:14*

RELATED QUESTION: *Are there angels in the room with us?*

NOTE TO PARENTS: *Some people think that each person has a guardian angel, an angel assigned to a person to watch over and protect him or her. We don't know for sure if people have guardian angels. But we do know that God uses angels to accomplish his will.*

Q: WHO IS THE DEVIL?

72

A: The devil is also called Satan. The word *devil* means "liar" or "enemy." Satan used to be an angel. But he wanted to be like God, so he fought against God. God kicked him out of heaven. Ever since then, Satan has worked on earth, trying to defeat God and God's people. He is God's enemy. But God is far stronger than Satan. In the end, Satan will be thrown into hell and suffer forever.

KEY VERSE: *But if you keep on sinning, it shows you belong to Satan. He has been sinning from the beginning. But the Son of God came to destroy the works of the devil. (1 John 3:8)*

RELATED VERSES: *Genesis 3:1-15; 1 Chronicles 21:1; Job 1:6-13; 2:1-7; Zechariah 3:1-2; Matthew 4:1-11; John 14:30; 2 Corinthians 11:14; Ephesians 6:11; Hebrews 2:14*

RELATED QUESTIONS: *Why did God make the devil? Why doesn't God kill Satan? Will God forgive Satan?*

Q: DOES THE DEVIL HAVE CLAWS?

73

A: The devil can take many forms. When he tempted Adam and Eve, he was a serpent. But remember, Satan is an angel and once was an angel of light. So he probably doesn't look like the funny costumes we see at Halloween (all red, with horns and a pitchfork). Instead, the devil usually tries to look like something good and beautiful. Remember, Satan is the father of lies, so he is usually trying to trick us. He'll say that we don't deserve to be God's children and that we are not forgiven. But always remember that God is much stronger than Satan (it's not even a close contest), and God can keep us safe from Satan.

KEY VERSE: *Yet I am not surprised! Satan can change himself into an angel of light. (2 Corinthians 11:14)*

RELATED VERSES: *Job 1:6-13; 2:1-7; Luke 11:4; John 8:44; James 4:7*

RELATED QUESTIONS: *Can the devil hurt me? Is the devil more powerful than God?*

NOTE TO PARENTS: *When children hear about Satan, they may wonder if he can hurt them physically. Of course that's possible, but Satan's attacks are usually much more subtle and focused on keeping people far from God. Usually he tries to get us to center our life around anything but God and to ignore God's commands. Explain to your child that God beats the devil every time and that we can beat Satan too (resist his temptations) if we stay close to God. This means doing what God says, relying on him, and talking to him about everything in our life.*

ANGELS AND DEMONS

Q: WHY IS THE DEVIL AFTER US?

74

A: Satan is God's enemy, so he is against anyone who is on God's side. Satan is jealous of our friendship with God—he can't stand it when we spend time with the Lord. And he wants to stop us from obeying God and from doing good. The devil hates God, so he hates us because we love God.

KEY VERSE: *So give yourselves humbly to God. Resist the devil and he will run from you. (James 4:7)*

RELATED VERSES: *Ephesians 6:11; 1 Peter 5:8-9; Revelation 12:9*

Q: WHAT ARE DEMONS?

75

A: Like the devil, demons are bad angels. They followed Satan when he turned against God. Demons are spiritual beings who work and fight against God. Demons are Satan's helpers. There is only one devil, but there are thousands of demons. They are all over the world, trying to keep people from following Christ and obeying God. But God is more powerful than all the demons and the devil put together. God will keep us safe from demons as we trust in him. At the end of time, all demons will be thrown into the Lake of Fire with the devil.

KEY VERSE: *[Jesus is speaking] "Then I will turn to those on my left. I will say, 'Away with you, you cursed ones. Go into the fire prepared for the devil and his demons.'" (Matthew 25:41)*

RELATED VERSES: *Mark 5:9-13; Luke 4:41; 11:15; Revelation 18:2*

NOTE TO PARENTS: *The related verses show that demons are active in the world.*

Q: WILL I EVER GET A DEMON?

76

A: It's easy to get the idea from watching television and hearing kids talk that demons can take over people's lives whenever they want. But that's not true. It is true that some people have demons in them. But demons can only enter people who let them and who are not close to God. And never forget, God is much more powerful than Satan or any of the demons. He can protect us.

KEY VERSES: *When the 70 disciples came back, they gave [Jesus] a joyful report. They said, "Even the demons obey us when we use your name." "Yes," he told them. "I saw Satan falling from Heaven like a flash of light! I have given you the power to walk among snakes and scorpions. And I have given you authority over the power of the Enemy. Nothing shall hurt you! But don't be full of joy because the demons obey you. Be full of joy because your names are written in Heaven." (Luke 10:17-20)*

RELATED VERSES: *Matthew 10:7-8; Romans 8:38-39*

SUFFERING
AND
EVIL

Q: WHY DO SOME PEOPLE DIE BEFORE THEY ARE OLD?

77

A: Death entered the world when sin came in. Ever since Adam and Eve, pain and death have been part of life. Eventually, everything that is alive in our world has to die. Plants die. Animals die. People die. Death can come from a lot of different causes: automobile accidents, sickness, old age, and so forth. And life is short, no matter how long a person lives. Just ask someone who is sixty or seventy or eighty. Remember that because life is short, we should make the most of every day we are alive. Each breath is a gift from God. But also remember that this life is not all there is. After we die we can live forever with God.

KEY VERSES: *For to me, living is Christ, and dying—well, that's better yet! But if I live I can win people to Christ. So I don't know which is better. Should I live or die? Sometimes I want to live, and at other times I don't. For I long to go and be with Christ. How much happier for me than being here! (Philippians 1:21-23)*

RELATED VERSE: *2 Corinthians 5:6*

Q: WHY ARE SOME PEOPLE DIFFERENT FROM OTHERS?

A: Bad things happen in this world, and people suffer. Some people are hurt in accidents. Some are injured in sports. Some are born with physical problems. You can probably think of many ways that people can be harmed. Today there are many doctors, nurses, and other people who can help us when we are hurt or need special help. They can give us medicine and bandages, and they can operate if necessary. And scientists are always working on special tools to help. Glasses, wheel chairs, hearing aids, and artificial legs are just a few of their wonderful inventions. These doctors and scientists are gifts from God.

KEY VERSES: *"Master," [Jesus'] disciples asked him, "why was this man born blind? Was it because of his own sins or those of his parents?" "Neither," Jesus answered. "He was born blind to show the power of God." (John 9:2-3)*

RELATED VERSES: *Matthew 5:4; 2 Corinthians 11:30; 12:8-10; 3 John 1:2*

RELATED QUESTION: *Why does God let people have disabilities?*

NOTE TO PARENTS: *God planned for people to be healthy. Disease, death, and disasters are a result of sin in the world. Everyone living in this sinful world suffers the effects of sin, even Christians. God may allow us to go through difficult times to teach us to rely on him or other lessons. Whatever our struggles, God can be glorified in them. In fact, God delights in demonstrating his strength in weak people.*

Q: HOW COME GOD MAKES STORMS WITH LIGHTENING AND THUNDER?

79

A: God made laws that control how the weather works. Thunder storms are part of our weather. Without rain, the grass, flowers, and crops wouldn't grow. The lightening and thunder in those storms come from the electricity in the air and on the earth. Of course, God can interrupt his laws of nature. But he made those laws so the earth would work. God doesn't send storms to scare us or hurt us. But storms can be dangerous, so we should stay out of their way and find cover when they come.

KEY VERSES: *The clouds poured down their rain. The thunder rolled and crackled in the sky. Your lightning flashed. There was thunder in the whirlwind. The lightning lighted up the world! The earth trembled and shook. (Psalm 77:17-18)*

RELATED VERSES: *1 Kings 18:5-45; Psalm 83:15*

RELATED QUESTIONS: *How come God makes weather hurt people or damage stuff? Does God make the weather every day?*

NOTE TO PARENTS: *As mentioned in the note for question 78, many natural disasters are the result of sin in the world. Of course we don't know all the reasons for hurricanes, earthquakes, tornadoes, and other terrible calamities. But some natural disasters are clearly the result of misusing the environment (for example, strip mining) or poor planning (for example, building on a flood plain).*

Q: WHY DOES GOD LET WARS HAPPEN?

80

A: Wars are a result of sin in the world. Because people aren't perfect, sometimes they get angry and fight. When leaders of countries do this, wars start. Wars are like fights between people, only much, much bigger. If people followed God's instructions for living, there would not be wars. God wants people to get along, not to fight and kill each other. But if we ignore God and break his rules, we suffer. God could stop all wars and fights in the world. But God wants human beings to trust him, to listen to him, to obey him, and to live in peace with each other.

KEY VERSES: *What is causing the fights among you? Isn't it because there is a whole army of evil desires within you? You want what you don't have. So you kill to get it! You long for what others have. So you start a fight to take it away! Why don't you have what you want? Because you don't ask God for it. (James 4:1-2)*

RELATED VERSES: *Matthew 24:6; 1 Corinthians 13:4-8*

RELATED QUESTION: *Does God make bad things happen?*

Q: WHY DOES GOD LET US GET SICK?

81

A: Sometimes sickness is the body's way of telling us that we should stop living a certain way. Perhaps we ate too much (or we ate something bad), or we didn't get enough sleep. Sickness and disease are problems that came into the world with sin. All kinds of people get sick: good and bad, rich and poor, old and young. God wants us to take care of ourself and be healthy so we can live for him. And when we are sick, we can pray to God and ask him to help us.

KEY VERSES: *Is anyone sick? He should call for the elders of the church. They should pray over him and pour a little oil upon him. They should call on the Lord to heal him. If their prayer is offered in faith, it will heal him. The Lord will make him well. If his sickness was caused by some sin, the Lord will forgive him. (James 5:14-15)*

RELATED VERSES: *Romans 5:3; 8:28; 2 Corinthians 12:8-9*

Q: IF WE ARE RUNNING OUT OF TREES, WHY DOESN'T GOD JUST MAKE MORE?

82

A: God *is* making more trees, but it is up to us not to use them faster than he replaces them. Some trees are cut down and used for wood, paper, and other products. Other trees are cut down to make room for houses, shopping centers, roads, and other construction projects. Some people say that we are running out of trees. When God created trees and other plants, he made them with the ability to make new ones. They do this by producing seeds that fall to the ground or are planted and then grow. But it takes many years for a tree to grow to be big and tall. So people should be careful not to cut down more trees than can be replaced by the seeds. God has given human beings the job of taking care of the earth. This includes using the trees wisely and planting new ones.

KEY VERSE: *Then God said, "Let us make a man—someone like ourselves. He will be the master of all life upon the earth and in the skies and in the seas." (Genesis 1:26)*

RELATED VERSES: *Deuteronomy 20:19; Revelation 7:3*

NOTE TO PARENTS: *Faithful stewards of the earth are sensitive to the environment. This kind of question is an opportunity for you to teach your children to take good care of God's earth and its resources.*

Q: DOES GOD KNOW ABOUT PEOPLE WHO ARE HUNGRY?

83

A: God knows everything. He even knows how many hairs you have on your head. God knows about all the hungry people in the world, and it makes him sad. Remember, he put *us* in charge of the world. God wants us to care about people and help those who need it. This includes helping to feed those who are hungry. Think about what you can do to feed the hungry people in your community.

KEY VERSES: *He is the God who made both earth and heaven. He made the seas and all that is in them. He is the God who keeps every promise. He gives justice to the poor. He gives food to the hungry. He sets the prisoners free. (Psalm 146:6-7)*

RELATED VERSES: *Matthew 10:29-31; Acts 27:34*

RELATED QUESTION: *Why doesn't God make enough food for everyone?*

Q: WHY DO BROTHERS AND SISTERS FIGHT?

84

A: Part of what it means to be a human being is to be sinful. In other words, no one in this world is perfect. We all do wrong things—we act in ways that displease God and that get us into trouble. Sinfulness causes us to get on each other's nerves and to get angry with one another. We even argue and fight with people we love, like our parents or our brothers and sisters. God has given us rules for living. If we follow his rules, we will get along with each other.

KEY VERSES: *At harvest time Cain brought the Lord a gift of his farm produce. Abel brought the fatty cuts of meat from his best lambs, and presented them to the Lord. The Lord accepted Abel's offering, but not Cain's. This made Cain dejected and very angry. His face grew dark with fury. "Why are you angry?" the Lord asked him. "Why is your face so dark with rage? It can be bright with joy if you will do what you should! But if you refuse to obey, watch out. Sin is waiting to attack you. It is longing to destroy you. But you can conquer it!" (Genesis 4:3-7)*

RELATED VERSES: *Genesis 4:8; James 4:1*

RELATED QUESTIONS: *Why are some people so mean? Why did God give me mean brothers and sisters?*

Q: WHY DO YOU GET MAD AT ME IF YOU HAVE JESUS IN YOUR HEART?

85

A: Not all anger is wrong. We should be angry with the bad things in the world, and we should try to make them right. When children disobey their parents and do other things that are wrong, sometimes their parents get angry. Good parents want their children to do what is right, and so they try to teach children right from wrong. Sometimes, of course, parents get angry at children for the wrong reasons. Maybe the parents are grouchy because they've had a bad day. Or maybe they misunderstood what their child did. Parents are human too; they can make mistakes. Even Christian parents who have God living in them and guiding them can do what is wrong at times. That happens when they don't do what God wants them to do. No matter how your parents act, you should love them and pray for them.

KEY VERSE: *If you are angry, don't sin by staying angry. Don't let the sun go down with you still angry. Get over it quickly. (Ephesians 4:26)*

RELATED VERSES: *Ecclesiastes 3:7-8; Romans 7:14; Colossians 3:5-8*

Q: WHAT IS EVIL?

86

A: Evil is another word for what is bad or sinful. Evil is anything that goes against God and displeases him. This includes a selfish attitude, bad actions, and ignoring God. Evil entered the world when Adam and Eve sinned in the Garden of Eden. You can read that story in the book of Genesis in the Bible. Ever since then, humans have been born wanting to do what is wrong. That's called our "sinful nature." So evil in the world comes from sinful human beings doing what comes naturally. Evil also comes directly from Satan. He is the enemy of God. The devil tries to get people to turn against God and disobey him. The good news is that we can overcome evil in ourself and in the world by giving our life to Jesus. God is far greater than Satan.

KEY VERSE: *Keep away from every kind of evil.* (1 Thessalonians 5:22)

RELATED VERSES: *Genesis 2:9; Matthew 12:34-35*

RELATED QUESTIONS: *What is sin? How do we displease God?*

THE
BIBLE

Q: HOW DID THEY WRITE THE OLD TESTAMENT IF THERE WEREN'T ANY PAPER OR PENCILS?

87

A: When the oldest books in the Bible were written, they didn't have typewriters, computers, or printing presses. And there weren't any ballpoint pens, felt-tipped pens, or number-two pencils. But the people who lived back then did have other tools for writing. The paper they used was different, too. The paper they first wrote the Old Testament on was probably either *papyrus* or *parchment*. Papyrus paper was made from a plant that grows in Bible lands. Parchment was made of animal skin. Either of these could be sewn into long pieces and rolled up into scrolls. Museums have some of these ancient scrolls. You may want to visit a museum and see one.

KEY VERSES: *After the king burned the scroll, the Lord spoke to Jeremiah. He said, "Get another scroll. Write everything again just as you did before." (Jeremiah 36:27-28)*

RELATED VERSES: *Exodus 24:12; 2 Timothy 4:13; 2 Peter 1:20-21*

Q: WHO WROTE THE BIBLE?

88

A: The words in the Bible came from God. That's why it is called "God's Word." God used people to write down the ideas, thoughts, teachings, and words that he wanted to put in the Bible. The writers were very special people, chosen by God for this very important task. And God used many people, writing over many, many years. These people wrote in their own style and in their own language, but they wrote God's Word. God guided their thoughts as they wrote. And God made sure that what they wrote was exactly what he wanted. He kept them from making any mistakes. Today we can read the Bible, God's Word, which he wrote through those special people so many years ago.

KEY VERSES: *No prophecy in the Bible was thought up by the prophet himself. The Holy Spirit within these godly men gave them true messages from God. (2 Peter 1:20-21)*

RELATED VERSES: *Exodus 31:18; 2 Timothy 4:13*

RELATED QUESTIONS: *How was the Bible made? Why did God ask certain people to write the Bible?*

Q: HOW DO WE KNOW THAT WHAT THE BIBLE SAYS IS TRUE?

89

A: The Bible is true because it is God's Word, and God always speaks the truth. When you read the Bible, you will see that it says it is the Word of God. The Bible also says that every word in it is true. But if that doesn't convince you, read the Bible and see for yourself that everything makes sense. When you read it, you will think, *This sounds right! This is true.* The Bible has also proven to be true over the many hundreds of years since it was written. For example, many events predicted in the Bible have happened, just as it said they would.

KEY VERSE: *The whole Bible was given to us by inspiration from God. It is useful to teach us what is true. It helps us to know what is wrong in our lives. It straightens us out and helps us do what is right. (2 Timothy 3:16)*

RELATED VERSES: *John 10:34-36; Hebrews 4:12; 2 Peter 3:15-16*

RELATED QUESTION: *Did the Bible stories really happen or are they like fairy tales?*

NOTE TO PARENTS: *Children usually will not raise this question as a matter of curiosity until they are older. Most will only ask a question like this if they are (1) mocked for believing the Bible, or (2) don't want to do something God wants them to do. If your children ask it, you might want to probe further before or after answering.*

Q: WHY DO WE HAVE THE BIBLE?

90

A: God gave us the Bible because he wanted to talk to us in a way that we would understand. Because God gave us his Word in a book, we can read it over and over. We can share it with a friend. The Bible is like a map—it shows us the direction to go in life. The Bible is like a love letter—it tells us about God's love for us. The Bible is like food—it gives us strength to live. To find out what God is like and how he wants us to live, read the Bible.

KEY VERSE: *For whatever God says to us is full of living power. It is sharper than the sharpest sword. It cuts swift and deep into our innermost thoughts and desires. It shows us for what we really are. (Hebrews 4:12)*

RELATED VERSES: *John 5:39-40; 16:13-15; 17:20; 20:30-31; Acts 17:11; 2 Timothy 3:16-17*

Q: WHY DO SOME BIBLES HAVE PICTURES AND SOME DON'T?

91

A: The people who wrote the Bible didn't put pictures in them. But in recent years, the people who print Bibles wanted to help us better understand the Bible stories. So they put pictures at various places in the Bible to help us see what Bible people and places may have looked like. The pictures are drawings or paintings, not photographs. These pictures were made recently—they're not very old. The artists knew what to draw by learning about that part of the world and by reading what the Bible says about how people lived in Bible times.

KEY VERSE: *When you come, bring the coat I left at Troas with Carpus. Also bring the books, but especially bring the parchments. (2 Timothy 4:13)*

RELATED VERSES: *2 Timothy 3:16-17*

RELATED QUESTION: *Why are there different Bibles?*

NOTE TO PARENTS: *In the key verse, Paul was in prison, just before his death when he wrote this letter to Timothy. The "parchments" were copies of the Old Testament Scriptures. With this question, children may also be asking why there are different versions of the Bible or why there is a difference between their Bible storybook and your Bible.*

Q: WHEN DID "BIBLE TIMES" STOP?

92

A: The last book in the Bible was written about seventy years after the time Jesus lived on earth. That's a very long time ago, almost two thousand years. In one way that's when Bible times stopped. But in other ways we are still in Bible times. God still speaks to us through his Word, he still cares about us, and he still does miracles. We may not see God divide a sea like he did for Moses, and we may not see anyone walk on water like Jesus did, but God still answers prayer and changes lives.

KEY VERSE: *Tell each other when you do wrong. Pray for each other. Then you will be healed. The earnest prayer of a righteous man has great power and wonderful results. (James 5:16)*

RELATED VERSES: *John 20:30-31; Hebrews 1:1-3; 4:7*

RELATED QUESTIONS: *How long ago was the Bible written? When was the Bible made?*

Q: WHY DID BIBLE PEOPLE GIVE THEIR KIDS SUCH FUNNY NAMES?

93

A: In ancient times, especially among the Jewish people, a person's name was very special. Usually it said something about the person or about the parents' dreams for their child. For example, Jedidiah means "lover of God." Sometimes God told prophets to give their children names with special messages. Hosea named his children Lo-ruhamah and Lo-ammi. Lo-ruhamah means "not loved," and Lo-Ammi means "not my people." By giving his children these unusual names, Hosea was giving God's message to the people. But usually names from other countries and cultures sound strange to us because we're not used to them. Names may sound funny to us, but not to the people in that country. Your name would probably sound funny to the people of Israel.

KEY VERSES: *Soon Gomer had another child. This one was a daughter. And God said to Hosea, "Name her Lo-ruhamah. This means 'No more mercy.' For I will have no more mercy upon Israel. I will not forgive her again. But I will have mercy on the tribe of Judah. I will free her from her enemies. I will do so without any help from her armies or weapons." Once Lo-ruhamah was no longer a baby, Gomer gave birth to a son. And God said, "Call him Lo-ammi. This means 'Not my people.' For Israel is not mine, and I am not her God." (Hosea 1:6-9)*

RELATED VERSES: *Genesis 30:8; 1 Samuel 25:25; Isaiah 8:1-4; Matthew 1:21*

Q: DOES SATAN KNOW ABOUT THE BIBLE?

94

A: Satan knows all about the Bible. He even knows what it says. But Satan certainly doesn't follow what the Bible teaches. In fact, he does everything he can to stop people from obeying God's Word. Just because someone knows the truth doesn't mean that he or she will do it. Satan is a liar, the father of lies. He has lied and twisted the truth so much that he has fooled himself into thinking that what the Bible predicts won't happen. Satan thinks that he can beat God and escape his punishment. But the Bible tells the truth. Eventually God will totally wipe out Satan and his demons.

KEY VERSES: *Are there still some among you who hold that "only believing" is enough? Is believing in one God enough? Well, remember that the demons believe this. And they shake with fear! Fool! Don't you know that "believing" is useless unless you do what God wants? Faith that does not result in good deeds is not real faith. (James 2:19-20)*

RELATED VERSES: *Matthew 4:6; John 5:39-40*

RELATED QUESTION: *If Satan knows the Bible, why doesn't he believe it?*

THE
CHURCH

Q: WHY DO WE GO TO CHURCH IF GOD IS EVERYWHERE?

95

A: In the Bible, God tells us to join other Christians and worship him. We should spend time alone, praying and reading his Word. But it is also very important to get together with others who follow Christ. We can encourage and strengthen each other. We can pray for each other. We can learn from each other. We can sing and praise God together. We can serve and help each other. All of this can happen in church. Church is also a place where Christians of all ages and types can come together—babies, grandparents, children, poor, wealthy, brown, black, white, American, Asian, African, weak, strong, and so on. Something very special happens when God's family gets together.

KEY VERSE: *Let us not neglect our church meetings, as some people do. Encourage and warn each other. Do this especially now that his day of coming is near. (Hebrews 10:25)*

RELATED VERSES: *1 Chronicles 16:29; Acts 2:42-47; 1 Corinthians 11:23-25; 12:12-31*

RELATED QUESTION: *Why do we have to go to church?*

NOTE TO PARENTS: *Many children find church boring. That's because the service is usually geared for adults. But it also may be because children have not been taught how to worship. Take time to explain the purpose behind the church programs (like Sunday school, church dinners, the worship service, and so forth) and each part of the worship service (for example, songs, Communion, offering, and so forth). Help your child understand what he or she should be doing and why.*

Q: WHY DO WE WORSHIP GOD?

96

A: Worship means praising and thanking God for who he is and for what he has done. People worship in many different ways. Worship can involve group singing, group reading, special music, giving money, prayer, Communion, Bible reading, teaching, preaching, and other activities. God has given us everything good that we have. He loves us and wants the very best for us. Shouldn't we spend time with him and tell him how grateful we are? We play with our friends because we enjoy them. We worship God because we enjoy him.

KEY VERSES: *Jesus replied, "Something new is coming. Then we will not worry about whether to worship here or in Jerusalem. For it's not where we worship that counts, but how we worship. We must worship in spirit and in truth. For God is Spirit, and we must worship him in truth." (John 4:21-24)*

RELATED VERSES: *Exodus 20:3; 1 Chronicles 16:29*

RELATED QUESTION: *Why do we have to do something that isn't fun?*

Q: HOW COME MY FRIENDS GO TO A DIFFERENT CHURCH?

97

A: In most homes, parents decide where children will go to church if they go. Some people go to a certain church because they grew up in that church. Even after moving across town, they drive there every Sunday to be with friends and family. Some people choose a church because they enjoy a certain style of worship. There are many reasons for choosing a church. But some churches really aren't true churches according to the Bible's teachings. Real churches honor Jesus, study God's Word, tell people to give their lives to Christ, and emphasize obeying God. Churches are groups of God's people, meeting together to worship, fellowship, serve, and learn.

KEY VERSES: *If someone says, "I love God," but hates his brother, he is a liar. He doesn't love his brother who is right there in front of him. So how can he love God whom he has never seen? And God said that one must love not only God but his brother too. (1 John 4:20-21)*

RELATED VERSES: *Acts 2:1; Hebrews 10:24-25*

RELATED QUESTION: *Why are there different types of churches?*

Q: WHAT PART OF THE BODY OF CHRIST AM I?

98

A: The Bible uses word pictures to explain how Christians relate to each other. We are a "family," with brothers and sisters in Christ. We are a "building," with Christ as the cornerstone. We are a "body," with each person serving as a special part. God talks about us being a body to show how Christians should treat each other and work together. God has given each Christian special gifts. That means each of us has talents and abilities that can be used to help other believers. Not everybody has the same gifts. And, like the parts of a body, we need each other. All of our gifts are important.

KEY VERSES: *There are many parts to our bodies. It is the same with Christ's body. We are all parts of his body. It takes every one of us to make it complete. We each have different work to do. We belong to each other, and each needs all the others. (Romans 12:4-5)*

RELATED VERSES: *Romans 12:6-8; 1 Corinthians 12:1-30*

NOTE TO PARENTS: *This is a question usually asked only by older children (junior high or older) who have heard teaching on the body of Christ. Encourage them to get involved with a gift or talent they have.*

Q: WHY DO PEOPLE GET BAPTIZED?

BAPTISMAL
TANK

99

A: People get baptized because Jesus was baptized, and they want to follow his example. They also get baptized because Jesus told his followers to go into all the world, telling people about him and baptizing them. Some Christians believe that babies from Christian families should be baptized to show that they belong to Christ. Some Christians think that only believers in Christ should be baptized, to show that Jesus is their Savior. Either way, baptism is a very important event in a Christian's life.

KEY VERSE: *And Peter replied, "Each one of you must turn from sin and come back to God. Then you must be baptized in the name of Jesus Christ. For through him, you will find forgiveness for your sins. Then you also shall be given this gift, the Holy Spirit." (Acts 2:38)*

RELATED VERSES: *Matthew 3:13-17; 28:19*

Q: WHAT HAPPENS TO PEOPLE WHO DON'T GO TO CHURCH?

100

A: Going to church doesn't get a person into heaven. And not going to church doesn't send a person to hell. A person becomes a Christian by faith—believing in Christ—not by doing good things. Most Christians go to church because of what happens there. At church you can meet other Christians. You can find help for your problems and encouragement. You can learn from God's Word and help others. And you can experience wonderful worship, singing, and praying that glorifies God. People who don't go to church miss all that. They miss a very special meeting with God.

KEY VERSES: *Then what can we brag about doing to earn our salvation? Nothing at all! Why? Because we were not forgiven because of our good deeds. Instead, we were forgiven because of what Christ has done and our faith in him. So we are saved by faith in Christ, not by the good things we do. (Romans 3:27-28)*

RELATED VERSES: *Ephesians 2:8-9; Hebrews 10:24-25*

RELATED QUESTION: *Does God send people to hell if they don't go to church?*

Q: WHEN IS JESUS COMING BACK?

101

A: Before Jesus left the earth many years ago, he promised to return some day. And after Jesus went up into the clouds, angels said he would come back eventually. No one knows exactly when that will happen. It could be any day now. For Christians, this is a wonderful event to look forward to. Christ's return will be the beginning of the end for Satan and all evil in the world. Won't it be great to see Jesus in person! Although no one knows when Christ will return, he told us to be ready. This means living the way he would want us to, using our time wisely, and telling others about God's Good News.

KEY VERSES: *[Jesus is speaking] "But no one knows the date and hour when the end will be. Not even the angels know this. No, not even God's Son knows this. Only the Father knows. . . . So be ready at all times. For you don't know what day your Lord is coming." (Matthew 24:36, 42)*

RELATED VERSES: *Matthew 24:27, 42-51; John 14:3; 1 Corinthians 1:7; Colossians 3:4; 1 Thessalonians 5:2-3; 2 Thessalonians 2:1-3; 2 Peter 3:12-13; Revelation 22:20*

RELATED QUESTION: *When can we really see Jesus?*